30 DAYS OF CHOICES
FOR SINGLE MOMS

Choices that bring hope and rekindle dreams

Lois M. Breit

Copyright © 2013 by Lois M. Breit

ISBN: 978-0-9887398-0-2

Editing by Sarah R Young

Cover by Matthew and Jill Reed

Special thanks to Laurene, Jamie, Heather, Melodee, and Jan. Your valued input and continuous encouragement kept this project alive.

All scripture quotations are from the New International Version, unless otherwise noted.

Printed in the United States of America

To Doug, Peter, Jill, Ben and Pamela.

*I am in awe of your ability to forgive
and your determination to overcome
life's challenges.*

INTRODUCTION

I've walked in your shoes, tasted your grief, felt your fears, and finally made choices that took me from victim to victor. My once out-of-control children have become responsible, caring adults who have chosen to follow God and His promises for their lives. Even so, I know you can do the best job possible as a parent, and your children may still choose to make bad decisions and choices themselves. As parents we can only teach and train our children to the best of our knowledge and ability. They will ultimately make their own choices. Let's do our part, and pray for God to help them do their part.

TODAY is a new day with new possibilities and maybe even new adventures. This day may be fraught with struggles, fears, and stress, or it may be a great memory-making day. Whichever you woke up to this morning, you have a choice to make. You can choose to be consumed by your unwanted circumstance, or you can begin to take steps away from those circumstances toward a better life. This may seem like an impossibility to you right now, but I encourage you to walk through this book one day at time and take the daily challenges presented. I really believe your life will change as you begin to dream about possibilities and promises instead of dwelling on your past or current circumstances.

MOMS, I hope reading this devotional book will help you make one new and good choice each day, choices that will restore hope and launch you into a new and better tomorrow.

Lois

*Day 1—*Choose to Read the Word, even if you're mad at God

Blessed is the man who does not walk in the counsel of the wicked or stand in the way of sinners or sit in the seat of mockers. But his delight is in the law of the Lord, and on His law he meditates day and night. He is like a tree planted by streams of water, which yields its fruit in season and whose leaf does not wither. Whatever he does prospers. —Psalm 1:1-3

Whether you're afraid, frustrated, or even still mad at God about your circumstances, choosing to read the Bible can help you find peace. Psalm 1:1-3 reminds us that good friends combined with sound scripture equals health and strength. If you choose to surround yourself with emotionally healthy people you gain strength. Critical people are draining and depressing. If you also read and meditate on scriptures of hope and promise, you'll be like "a tree planted by streams of water"—in a healthy place to mature and flourish. A healthy tree produces fruit, and in your case, the fruit of God's Spirit—love, joy, peace, patience, kindness, gentleness and self-control. Because the tree is healthy, "its leaf does not wither"—you will no longer feel dry and dead inside. It ends with the best promise of all— "whatever he does prospers"— the blessings of God.

Today, read Scripture, choose to surround yourself with healthy people, and prepare yourself for the challenges of your day with the hope of a better tomorrow.

Nights were always the hardest for me. The end of the day gave me time to think and rehash the breakdown of my marriage. I decided to take a Bible course (a Bible study would be just as good), with Bible reading homework. This took my mind off my problems and helped me focus on God's Word, promises and hope.

Day 2—Choose to get out of bed this morning

Because of the Lord's great love we are not consumed, His compassions never fail, they are new every morning, great is Your faithfulness. —Lamentations 3:22–23

I know you may want to stay in bed today, pull the covers over your head, and wish your circumstances were different, but none of that will take away your grief or change your situation.

Re-read the opening line of this passage as if God were speaking directly to you. *Because of the Lord's great love [for me], I am not consumed!* Stop right there. God is telling you two important things here.

First of all, He has a great love for you! Whether you accept His love, believe His love exists, or choose to reject His love, God will still love you. That can't change, no matter what you do, or think you've done to annoy Him!

He goes on to say that your problems do not need to consume you. When something is consumed, it is devoured or destroyed. Sound familiar? It's what makes us want to quit, give up, and not get out of bed in the morning. You may be wondering: How can God's love possibly stop the all-consuming issues I have to face once again today? That's a good question.

You may have awakened this morning feeling very alone, wishing for someone who cared, who could help, or even someone who just understands what you are facing today. Well, being loved by God means someone does care! When you accept His love, a feeling of value, confidence, and hope overtakes you. Your battles will seem less overwhelming.

God doesn't stop with telling you how much He loves you and that you don't need to be consumed by your circumstances. He goes on to remind you that He is also filled with compassion. Webster's Dictionary defines compassion as "a feeling of deep sympathy and sorrow for another who is stricken by misfortune, *accompanied by* a strong desire to alleviate the suffering." The longer we blame God for our problems, the more they consume us. God is not the cause of our suffering—He is actually the answer to alleviate it!

Family and friends can tire of our problems and emotional fluctuations, but God will never tire because *"His compassions never fail, they are new every morning."* He is ready and waiting each morning with a fresh love, a fresh compassion, and a fresh ear to hear.

This scripture ends with these powerful words of promise: "great is Your [God's] faithfulness". As a single mother, you need someone who will be steady, trustworthy, and faithful to you (definition of faithful: true to one's word, promises, vows).

You may still have a court appearance today, a rebellious teen to deal with, a job you hate, or a bill that is due. Problems don't go away. But you can be confident that you are not alone. God will give you the strength and courage you need to face your challenges and the wisdom you need to resolve them.

From beginning to end, this scripture from God is saying the words we long to hear: *I love you. I care about you. I can help you. I'll listen to you. Today is a new day, and no matter what you face, I will be with you. I will be faithful, always.*

So get up, brush your teeth, fix your hair, stand up tall, and begin to walk through your crazy, hectic, stressful day knowing you are greatly loved by a God who desires to restore your life and your home, one day at a time.

~

I remember when I had to drag myself out of bed and try to face another day. I didn't want to get up because my days were too hard, too empty, too lonely, and I felt so unloved. Getting out of bed became easier after Lamentations 3:22–23 became a reality to me.

Day 3—Choose to Trust once again

Some trust in chariots and some in horses, but we trust in the name of the LORD our God.—Psalm 20:7

Okay, I know your chariot is not sitting outside your door this morning, and your horse may have escaped from the garage. So what does this scripture mean for you today, and what does it have to do with trusting God?

In biblical days, when a battle was being waged, those with the strongest horses and most sturdy chariots faced their enemies with confidence and often won the war. This verse says horses and chariots are fine, but we need something more powerful for our daily battles. A horse cannot defeat a battle of the mind, pocketbook, or illness. The strongest chariot cannot keep up with the frustrations of the day or the fears that come at night. We need something beyond our own resources to find the victories we seek.

As a single mother, you face a battle almost every day. It might be a small battle of the wills or a large legal battle that looms in front of you. You may be searching for a new job, apartment, or car. What or whom are you trusting for your victory?

Strong horses and chariots were a real asset in historical times, just like a good lawyer, education, or friend may be today. However, if you are not putting your trust in God first and foremost, your victories will be limited, because man is limited.

Trust doesn't come easily, I know. Most single moms have had an intimate trust broken or betrayed. Trusting God may be even more difficult after you've prayed for a physical or relational healing that didn't come to be. However, if we only trust when we get what we want, there is little faith involved.

When trust is broken, we often withdraw and turn to a form of self-sufficiency, trusting only our own abilities. We will ask for help only when forced to, such as when a court appearance requires a lawyer. Some give up on themselves and God and look to a program for their provision rather than the Lord. Some single moms read magazines and statistics that reinforce their fears instead of the Bible that will instill hope and trust. We make trust choices every day.

As you make your way through the day, think about whom or what you are trusting when making decisions, facing conflict, or considering personal choices.

～

My faith and trust in God were shaken to the core when my husband left me to raise our five children alone. I found it very difficult to trust a God who had "allowed" this devastation to overtake me. However, when I quit blaming God for the choices and behaviors of others, I found trusting Him much easier. I endured because trust restored my peace; God's faithfulness never failed.

Day 4—Choose to believe God really exists

And without faith it is impossible to please God, because anyone who comes to Him must believe that He exists and that He rewards those who earnestly seek Him. —Hebrews 11:6

When we feel God has ignored our pleas for help, healing, or the restoration of a relationship, it's hard to believe God is really there, that He exists at all.

Faith, as defined by Webster's Dictionary, is "a belief that is not based on proof, but it is confidence or trust in a person or thing." We have a lot of faith when things are going well, but seem to have little or no faith when things don't go as we want or expect. Suddenly we think God must not exist, or He becomes the target of our blame.

If you believe today that God truly exists, that He cares about your well-being even though you are not feeling "well" at the moment, you have faith. This scripture says you will be rewarded if you have faith, if you believe He exists.

The Bible doesn't say that life will always be fair for the believer, or that we will understand everything that happens. On the contrary—it says, "expect trials and trouble." Yet when those trials come, especially in the form of a loss, we say God doesn't exist or it's His fault we are suffering.

I often think of the blind man Jesus and the disciples came

across. In John 9:2, the disciples asked Jesus *"Rabbi, who sinned, this man or his parents, that he was born blind?" "Neither this man nor his parents sinned," said Jesus, "but this happened so that the works of God might be displayed in him."*

This doesn't tell me God wanted the man to be blind, only that God would use his blindness to glorify Himself. God has a bigger picture of our lives and our world than we will ever be able to imagine.

God cares about character, integrity, and faithfulness. We care about our personal comfort and never having to suffer loss. God always has His eye on our eternal future and well being, while we only have eyes for this earthly life. Jesus expects us to grieve, and He understands our pain. However, He offers encouragement with these words from 1 Thessalonians 4:13: *"Brothers and sisters, we do not want you to be uninformed about those who sleep in death, so that you do not grieve like the rest of mankind, who have no hope."*

Today you can be rewarded with peace, comfort, or whatever else is lacking, just by coming to God and believing that He really exists. He is listening. He does care. Try reading Hebrews 11:6 out loud, and believe God is listening to you. Choose to believe God really exists, even if you don't feel His presence at the moment, and remember, He rewards those who earnestly (continuously) seek Him on the good days and the bad.

At one point, my world seemed so black and so empty, without hope or future. But when I read these scriptures and chose to believe God existed, even if I didn't feel Him, see Him, or fully understand Him, I began to move forward, reaching for His hope. Though I felt as if I were in a very dark tunnel, stumbling around, I held on to God's promise for light at the end of my tunnel. I just had to keep walking toward it, in faith, believing the light was there, even when I couldn't' see it. Eventually the day came when a pinprick of light began to appear, and eventually my tunnel became brighter. When we choose to have faith in God, believing that He really exists and cares about us, we stumble less, become steady in our emotions, and sometimes are surprised by how close we are to the tunnel's opening.

*Day 5—*Choose Kind words today

The words of the reckless pierce like swords, but the tongue of the wise brings healing —Proverbs 12:18

Gracious words are a honeycomb, sweet to the soul and healing to the bones. —Proverbs 16:24

When things don't go our way or when frustrations build, we can spew reckless words without thinking. I've often wondered how we might change our vocabulary and our tone if we could actually hear ourselves throughout the day. I think it could be quite an embarrassing experience.

These scriptures speak such truth! How many times have someone's words pierced your heart, made you feel inferior, or left you defeated? In Romans 7:15, Paul wrote these famous words, *"I decide one way, but then I act another, doing things I absolutely despise" (The Message).* We follow our human nature all too often. We hate when someone speaks harsh words to us, or uses a tone that hurts, and yet we do this very same thing to those we love.

Today, if your voice is raised, filled with anger or malice, with impatience brimming over, refrain from speaking until you are calm. Choose to say only words that edify, encourage, or correct with gentleness, or choose to say nothing at all—close your mouth! Yes, you can do this.

Today, ponder this scripture and choose to speak with words that heal rather than pierce.

I punished my sons whenever they said bad words or were disrespectful. But when I think back, my hurtful, angry, and sometimes raging words deserved punishment as much as their inappropriate words. You will live with fewer regrets if you can calm yourself before verbally responding to your children and others.

*Day 6—*Choose to join a small group or Bible study

Let us consider how we may spur one another on toward love and good deeds, not giving up meeting together, as some are in the habit of doing, but encouraging one another—and all the more as you see the Day approaching. —Hebrews 10:24–25

Too often, as single moms, we isolate ourselves. We feel we do not measure up and that we will not be accepted. We let these and other thoughts control our minds and keep us away from people. But God created us to be a "family.".

God knows we need each other for encouragement, for love, and for thinking outside of ourselves. Choose to become part of something bigger than yourself today. Ask about small groups at your local church, and then be brave enough to go to one. Attend at least four times before dropping out. Give them a chance, and give yourself a chance to find new friends, a new voice, a new ear, and maybe even a new outlook on life.

My first small group was a disaster. The first meeting I was told children were welcome. After I attended once (with my five kids), I was told children were no longer welcome and that I'd need to find a babysitter. The people were judgmental (or maybe I was?). They were dogmatic, lacked love, and projected an attitude of superiority. So I quit going and became more isolated. I felt even more unwanted and left out. Then I chose to try a different group within the same church. This group was of varied ages and backgrounds, but they were the right group for me. I stayed with that group for years. They became my friends and mentors. They taught me to trust again and were a living and practical example of healthy relationships.

*Day 7—*Choose to control your temper

The one who has knowledge uses words with restraint, and whoever has understanding is even-tempered.— *Proverbs 17:27*

I love the first half of this verse: "The one who has knowledge uses words with restraint." This tells us two things. First of all, the person has taken time to gain knowledge about a situation before reacting. A wise person seeks understanding and responds with restraint, choosing not to have an emotional outburst. Too many times, children, family, or friends are left in the wake of a single mother's rants.

How do we gain knowledge, use restraint, and become even-tempered? It gets easier if we ask questions, don't let frustrations build, avoid triggers, and gain composure before responding.

Being even-tempered and using the right words will take self-discipline. We must gather all the information we can before reacting and responding. We cannot let fear or anger escalate a situation. A poor response cannot be justified with a lame excuse. When on the edge of an eruption, our choice must be to leave the room, take a walk, and say a prayer before responding. Make a conscious effort to stop yourself *before* you lose control of your temper and your words!

We often lose our temper when we allow our children free reign with their mouths or attitudes. If your child relentlessly disobeys or challenges you, be firm with your response at the beginning and follow through with established punishments. Discipline can be exercised with calm, kind, correcting words; we do not need to yell, scream, and curse to accomplish our goals. Know when to walk away, when to discipline, and when to lighten up and laugh.

A reaction is quick and sharp, the result of a lost temper. A response is thought out and executed with restraint, the result of an even temper. When we gain understanding as to why we rage, we can begin to take control of our temper and responses.

Today choose to assess your trigger points, gain all the information you can about what's made you angry, and then gain control of your emotions before responding.

~

I was tired, angry, and full of excuses for my short temper until I finally chose to change me. I assessed some of the things that raised my pressure level, like keeping the house clean all the time. I had set unrealistic goals and it had become a pressure point for the entire family. Impressing outsiders had taken precedence over enjoying my children. The pressure was relieved when I chose to play with my children more and clean the house less. I also looked at what behaviors caused me to explode with anger, like the repeated defiance of my children. I gained control of my temper when I chose to discipline immediately rather than argue with or ignore their behavior until we were all out of control.

Day 8—Choose to accept forgiveness for yourself

Therefore, there is now no condemnation for those who are in Christ Jesus —Romans 8:1

It is finished. —John 19:30

Ever wake up hating yourself, kicking yourself for words you've said or things you've done? For some single moms, that's a daily routine. We find no value in ourselves because we have taken the blame for everything that has gone wrong in our lives. Maybe you have made some bad choices, or said words you can never take back. That's true for every person who lives and breathes on this earth. But when regret dominates our thoughts, forward motion usually comes to a halt.

When Jesus died on the cross for the sins of mankind, it included your sins as well. He said, "It is finished" because there was nothing else that needed to be done for *all of us* to be forgiven and brought back into relationship with God. First John 1:9 says it another way: "If we confess our sins, He is faithful and just and will forgive us our sins and purify us from all unrighteousness." If you've sincerely asked God to forgive you, then you *are* forgiven.

You will continue to feel depressed, unworthy, and even ugly when you live in a state of guilt or self-condemnation. However, hope, joy, and vision return when you accept the forgiveness God has extended to you.

So today, choose to ask for forgiveness if you have not yet done so. Then believe you are forgiven, quit looking at past mistakes, and start planning for future opportunities. "Now there is no condemnation," so let it go. "It is finished," so accept God's gift of forgiveness today.

~

When I was living at the bottom of my dark, depressed pit, I felt very hopeless. I was hopeless because I felt worthless, worthless because I couldn't forgive myself for past mistakes (both real and imagined). I lived with guilt and condemnation for things I'd said and not said, done and not done. This is familiar territory for most women. I just couldn't forgive myself or quit blaming myself for being a failure. Then I read these scriptures. I wondered how someone with my low self-esteem could think she was somehow so special that Christ's sacrifice on the cross was not enough for me. I just didn't deserve forgiveness. But who does? Did God really have to do something special just for me, above and beyond what He did for the rest of mankind? Self-hatred is always destructive. Compassion and forgiveness are always healing.

Day 9—Choose to be responsible (self-disciplined)

Do you not know that in a race all the runners run, but only one gets the prize? Run in such a way as to get the prize.
—*1 Corinthians 9:24*

For the Spirit God gave us does not make us timid, but gives us power, love, and self-discipline. —*2 Timothy 1:7*

For lack of discipline they will die, led astray by their own great folly. —*Proverbs 5:23*

Today is the day to look in the mirror, fix your hair, put on your makeup, get to work on time, give no excuses, and devise a plan of action.

As a single mom, it's easy to let things slide. We let emotions rule our days rather than the need to be the responsible adult. You're too busy, too tired, too sad, or too darn mad at your circumstances!

It's time to choose to discipline yourself. What does that mean?

It's different for each of us, but let's begin with the basics:

- Get up on time.

- Get up with a good attitude.

- Prepare for your day the night before. This may mean

making sure all homework is done and backpacks are ready, clothes are laid out (including yours), lunches are made, and your alarm clock is set earlier than your child's.

If you've got this part of your day under control, you're ready for phase two:

- Read one or two scriptures (or a devotional) to get your mind in the right attitude for your day.

- Do not over-schedule. Cut out or cut down on extra curricular activities. Be choosy about what your children (and you) are involved in. Be the mom and set the boundaries. They may want to do everything, but you are only one person and limits need to be set *by you.*

- Be consistent in disciplining your children. That means following through every time, making no idle threats (anything you won't or can't follow through on), and getting off the couch, off the phone, or away from your task to follow through. Let your children know you mean what you say, and only say what you mean.

- Be true to your word. Do not promise what you cannot fulfill, and be a person of integrity.

Self-discipline does not happen overnight. It's an ongoing process and will proceed according to the effort you put in to it.

So, today, choose one thing on this list, or your own list, that will help you become more disciplined. Once established as a habit, move on to another throughout this month. You can do it!

~

I hated getting up so early every morning! I cried when my alarm went off and then rushed like a maniac to get us all ready for school and work. I finally decided to quit being sad and begin to be responsible. I chose to face my circumstances and give my children every opportunity to succeed. My self-discipline and new attitude changed my life and theirs.

Day 10—Chose to forgive others (as God forgives you)

Bear with each other and forgive one another if any of you has a grievance against someone. Forgive as the Lord forgave you.
—*Colossians 3:13*

Okay, I know this is a hard choice to make. However, if it weren't important, God would not have given us scriptures like these to follow. Forgiveness clears our history, restores our vision, and most importantly, releases us from the control of others. When we do not forgive, we are left bitter, spiteful, and angry, and these emotions spill out in our words and actions.

Forgiveness breaks the power of demoralizing words, recurring thoughts, and controlled behaviors. You will be changed and empowered, and you'll find peace when you forgive. An offender might be changed because of your act of forgiveness, but most likely will not ever know, care, or understand it. This choice is for you!

Forgiveness is a choice, not an emotion. You choose to forgive so you can find peace. You choose to forgive so your children will learn to be compassionate and forgiving (you will need their forgiveness from time to time, too). You choose to forgive because God has forgiven you. You are not letting someone off the hook for their behavior when you forgive, you are actually gaining control of your own life and future. An offender no longer has power over your choices, confidence, emotions, or future when you forgive. Let it go!

The life-changing freedom that comes with forgiving others will take some time because offenders are often in our lives for years. But choose to begin or continue this process of forgiving today, and your day will be much happier.

~

Until I could forgive those who had hurt me, I could not move forward with my life. I was stuck in my pain, frustrations, and anger. I kept waiting for people and circumstances to change. Their hurtful words and actions seemed to control my every thought. When I reluctantly chose to forgive and to give up my "right" to be angry, my reactions to life and my children changed dramatically.

I began by saying out loud: "I choose to forgive (name) for (offense)" every time I was hurt or angered. Speaking these words of forgiveness to God, not my offender, didn't mean I left myself vulnerable to my offender's behavior. On the contrary, those words actually broke my offender's power over me, and I was no longer controlled by what he said or did. This choice to forgive kept me from passing bitter attitudes on to my children. It took hate and anger out of our home and put love back into it.

Day 11—Choose to give, not just take

As Jesus looked up, He saw the rich putting their gifts into the temple treasury. He also saw a poor widow put in two very small copper coins. "Truly I tell you," He said, "this poor widow has put in more than all the others. . —Luke 21:1–3

Give, and it will be given to you. A good measure, pressed down, shaken together and running over, will be poured into your lap. For with the measure you use, it will be measured to you. — Luke 6:38

Are you in need today? Maybe it's a need for more money, food, time, patience, or love. The fact is, we all wake up with needs. Ask yourself if you've noticed anyone else in need the past week or month. If not, you are probably being consumed by your problems and have lost the joy of giving to others in need.

How can you give today, even if *you* are in great need? Look at the homeless person on the corner, the person next to you on the bus, the other harried mother rushing in to school with her child, or the coworker who has seemed exceptionally sad or moody. Give the homeless a dollar, say hello to the person on the bus, speak a kind word of encouragement to the rushed mother, serve a cup of coffee to the coworker. The smallest gesture of compassion can be the biggest blessing to someone in need.

Even as you face your own tight budget, God wants you to see the needs of others. The woman who gave her pennies gave from her heart to help others, trusting God would meet her needs.

We all like to receive, but through these scriptures, God is trying to show us the importance of giving as well.

We teach our children to be independent, confident, and generous adults through our giving. We receive the blessings of God, according to His promises, through our giving. We will remain compassionate and caring, aware of the needs of others, by giving.

Today, choose to give something of importance to someone in need. It could be an article of clothing for a friend, a batch of cookies for a lonely neighbor, or a few sacrificial coins for the offering plate.

When I was overrun with problems and quite penniless myself, I chose to give of myself to our church. I began by learning to run the sound system for our evening services. I could stay hidden in the balcony and yet give to my church where they had a need. I also helped a neighbor who had Multiple Sclerosis do her grocery shopping. These were ways I could give to others, become more confident in myself, and get my mind off my own problems and notice the needs of others.

Becoming a giver also impacted my children. They received a

lot of their clothing from bags given by generous, anonymous donors. Whenever they received "new" clothes, they chose a selection from their old clothes to pass on to someone else. They understood the joy of giving as much as the pleasure of receiving. Because they were givers, they didn't view themselves as poor.

My daughter taught her dorm floor how to give their best in a clothing drive her freshman year. Because she had received clothes as a child from such benefits, she asked the girls if they would want to receive the torn, stained clothing they were putting into the clothing box. The girls took back their worn out clothes and sacrificially gave quality items instead.

Day 12—Choose to wisely discipline your child (don't give up)

Fathers, do not exasperate your children; instead, bring them up in the training and instruction of the Lord. . —Ephesians 6:4

Whoever spares the rod hates their children, but the one who loves their children is careful to discipline them.
—Proverbs 13:24

The wise in heart are called discerning, and gracious words promote instruction. . —Proverbs 16:21

When you exasperate your children, you become weary yourself. If you let issues slide and avoid discipline, your home becomes chaotic. These three scriptures are meant to instruct us as parents so we can correctly train and discipline our children.

Don't be afraid to discipline. Learn to be consistent, firm, wise, and calm. That's a big order, but if you tackle just one of these aspects at a time, you will soon merge them together as a whole, healthy way to discipline.

Ideas for disciplining your children:

- Explain the new rules and punishments so your kids know what to expect when rules are broken or defied.

- Give only one warning with a reminder of the consequence.

- Follow through after that one warning. Do not continue to warn, threaten, or discuss options— follow through! When a child learns they cannot manipulate or outlast you, angry exchanges are avoided and children quickly begin to obey because they believe the consequence will follow.

- Do not punish when you're angry. Calm yourself first.

- Remember who is in charge—that would be you!

You may not feel strong, brave, or full of discernment today, but choose not to give up on your children. They need you, even when you are worn out. Be vigilant in preparing them for their future and bringing order to your home.

Make one brave decision today regarding the discipline of your children and stop making excuses for their bad behavior to yourself and others.

~

I remember when my rebellious 13-year-old son insisted a schoolmate was not loved by his parents. After some discussion about why he felt this way about a boy he knew only by facial recognition from school, he totally surprised me with his reasoning. He said, "Well, Tommy is out skating at the park right now, and he was expelled from school. If I were expelled from school, you would ground me for life! His parents can't love him, because they don't care what he's doing." The son I grew tired of punishing actually understood he was being punished because he was loved!

Day 13—Choose joy

Worship the LORD with gladness; come before Him with joyful songs. —Psalm 100:2

"At that time," declares the LORD, "I will be the God of all the families of Israel, and they will be My people." . . . Then young women will dance and be glad, young men and old as well. I will turn their mourning into gladness; I will give them comfort and joy instead of sorrow. —Jeremiah 31:1, 13

Today you may think there is nothing to be joyful about. The washing machine may be broken, the car in need of repair, your child unhappy you said "no" to something, and the bus—once again—much too early! These are life's realities. However, this passage in Jeremiah is a reminder that, even when we pass through hard times, God desires to restore our joy. He knows how important joy is to our lives. Without joy we are empty, hopeless, muddled in our thinking, reactionary instead of rational, and worst of all, just plain sad.

God is reminding us that we are His children, His family. But even as God's family, we bump into life and face hard times. Sometimes it's because of our own choices, sometimes because of others. Most often, it's because we live in an imperfect world with imperfect people. I love that God says we are His family—we will survive. He loves us, He will rebuild our lives, we will flourish once again, and best of all—He will see us "dance with the joy."

Melancholy days make it hard to believe God's words of promise or hope for joy. The darkness can surround us and make it difficult to make positive choices. But our choices always have and always will dictate our final action.

Even on a melancholy day, sing a song that makes you smile, plan a surprise for your child, skip a task you dread, or write a note of thanks to someone. Choosing to do the things that bring joy is our way of responding to God's promise and beginning our journey to joy.

~

There were many days I burst into tears over the smallest memory or moment of stress. I learned to just cry out my emotion, take a deep breath, trust God was working in my out-of-control life, and find a thought that would bring me a small amount of joy. A small choice can bring a large result.

Day 14—Choose to be happy and put a smile on your face

A happy heart makes the face cheerful, but heartache crushes the spirit. . —Proverbs 15:13

I challenge you to choose to be happy today, and I know how difficult that can be.

So let's start with the easy things. Is the sun shining? Do you have a child you love? Do you have a job? Is it a pleasant summer day, or a beautiful winter day? Do you have a good best friend? Do you have good health? At least one of these things should be a yes!

Put on your favorite pair of shoes. Plan your favorite meal for dinner. Think of one little treat you can give yourself today. Give your kids extra hugs. If they are ornery, laugh it off and know they will out-grow this stage, too. Put on a worship CD while you get ready for work or get the kids ready for school. Sing along, even if you don't feel like it. Worship brings peace to both body and soul.

You can always find the negatives and disappointments in your day, *but not today*! Today, choose to worship the Lord with gladness, come before Him with joyful songs. Not because your day is perfect, but because you have God's promise for better days.

Today, make a tally card for the good in your day, not your disappointments, and choose to smile at least once today!

~

The first six months after my husband left, I woke up to extreme sadness everyday. I'm sure everyone I knew was tired of me, but I just couldn't seem to pull myself out of grief mode. One day I looked at my kids with new eyes, I realized they needed me to laugh again and bring joy back into our home. The time for grieving, anger, sadness, and just waiting for life to be the way I wanted it had to come to an end. It was my first day of choosing to be happy about things in my day instead of just seeing the problems. My kids would say, "Smile, Mama," and I'd reply, "I am." They would say, "You're not smiling with your face." They needed to see joy, not just be told it was there. This is a good reminder for all of us.

Day 15—Chose to love again

Blessed is the one who always trembles before God, but whoever hardens their heart falls into trouble. —Proverbs 28:14

When we tremble before God, we remember His position, His power, and His majesty. We don't fight against Him, but we humble ourselves before Him. Those who do not fear God tend to rebel against Him. For some that means rejection of faith, but for others it means shutting people out by hardening their hearts against love.

A hard heart is trouble because it ruins relationship, and God is all about relationship. He knows relationship is what binds us to Himself and what makes life on this earth enjoyable. Relationships are limited without love. To love means to trust and to trust means to forgive, and forgiveness means we have healed hearts.

We were created to be loved and to love others. If our hearts become hard, we close off the possibility of love. If you think you are protecting yourself from further hurt by keeping people at arm's length, you are actually doing the opposite. When we harden our hearts, we become dead in our spirits, in our motivation, and in our emotions. To "tremble before God" means we trust Him and find safety in Him, not in the walls we try to build ourselves.

If you've closed your heart to those around you, today can be the start of a new day. Just do one kind thing for a family member or friend. It can be as simple as buying a candy bar you know they like or giving them a hug. We must "feel" if we are to live and enjoy life.

I joined a Bible study several months after my husband left. The leaders of the small group were 20 years older than me and I learned so much from them. I became very good friends with this couple, and Elsie taught me to trust again. Every time I left her home, she'd say, "I love you." I always respond with, "Yeah, see you later". After a couple of years of this, it dawned on me that I just couldn't say, "I love you" back to her. In my quest to never be hurt again, I'd made a vow to wall off my feelings for people, and never love anyone again—my heart had hardened. But I chose to do something about this hard-hearted condition. I made a new choice, to respond with "I love you" the next time I left her home. It was hard for me to say it the first time, but soon it became hard not to say those words of endearment. My heart began its healing process and my emotional troubles began to subside after I made the choice to love again.

Day 16—Choose Life

The thief comes only to steal and kill and destroy; I have come that they may have life, and have it to the full. —John 10:10

This day I call the heavens and the earth as witnesses against you that I have set before you life and death, blessings and curses. Now choose life, so that you and your children may live and that you may love the LORD your God, listen to His voice, and hold fast to Him. —Deuteronomy 30:19–20

Despondency leads to hopelessness, which leads to thoughts of death. It doesn't have to be suicide, though it often is. The desire to live ebbs, and thoughts of death seem comforting. If you are suffering from severe depression or suicidal thoughts, seek professional help immediately. The more we play with thoughts of death, the more inviting they become. These thoughts are contrary to God's will for our lives.

Satan is a thief who wants to kill and destroy. God wants to give us life, and abundant life at that. We weren't created to just exist, but to exude life itself. In times of grief, we will not be bouncing off the walls with joy, but neither should we grieve to the point of giving up on life.

It's work to choose life when our circumstances are hard, when giving up seems much easier. Life takes effort and quitting does not, but God is asking you to choose life. Begin here.

- Eat right—sugar can exacerbate or deepen depression.

- Talk to a happy friend today—avoid the negative people.

- Take a walk—it will relieve stress and depression.

- Make a doctors appointment—be assured you are healthy.

- Don't look back today—think of something you'd like to do in the future.

You may be feeling like life is over, but it's not! Today, make choices that will help pull your mind away from death and defeat and on to life.

~

I, too, have felt life was over. I prayed each night to die in my sleep so I wouldn't have to face another painful, sad day. But soon the thoughts of death began to dominate me. One night I felt God say to me, "You are willing to die for Me, but are you willing to live for Me?" I couldn't answer that question. I knew that death was easy—I could just give up and get weaker and weaker until I faded away. Life meant I'd have to change my thoughts, attitudes, outlook, and actions. But after debating this choice for a few days, I chose life and never looked back. God has taken me on an amazing adventure of life since I made that decision. He desires to do the same for you!

Day 17—Choose to control your thoughts

We demolish arguments and every pretension that sets itself up against the knowledge of God, and we take captive every thought to make it obedient to Christ. —2 Corinthians 10:5

Do you believe you are ugly or worthless? Is your life controlled by fear and anxiety? Does your mind constantly replay all of your mistakes? Today is the day to "take captive every thought and make it obedient to Christ." But how?

You must read your Bible to understand how God views you, why He created you, and the hope and purpose He *always* has for you. Without these truths from God's Word, you are powerless to take your thoughts captive or destroy their power over your mind and emotions. With this knowledge comes the power to speak truth to the lies. For example:

What You Think	**Scripture Truth**
I'm stupid.	"I have the mind of Christ." 1 Corinthians 2:16
I'm not lovable.	"I love you with an everlasting love." Jeremiah 31:3
Nobody is on my side.	"If God is for us, who can be against us?" Romans 8:31
I can't be forgiven.	"As far as the East is from the West, so far have I removed your transgressions [sins/mistakes] from you." Psalm 103:12

You take captive destructive thoughts and make them obedient to Christ by making sure they agree with God's view of you, as spoken through His Word. God is for you, He loves you, and He desires good things for you!

Today, take one negative thought that seems to control your actions and look for a scripture that crushes that lie. You may need to ask a Christian friend or pastor to help you get started on this journey of finding truth and demolishing lies. A great book on the topic is *Telling Yourself the Truth* by William Backus and Marie Chapian.

~

I believed for a long time that I was ugly, unlovable, worthless, a failure, and stupid. I lived with great fear, even to the point of anxiety attacks. I was waiting for the next bad thing to happen to me or my family. My life changed after I read Telling Yourself the Truth, accepted forgiveness for myself, and believed God's promises were for me. I was able to take captive the lies that ran through my head, demolish the stronghold of fear, and move toward a future God had planned for me.

Day 18—Choose to hope

Against all hope, Abraham in hope believed and so became the father of many nations, just as it had been said to him, "So shall your offspring be." —Romans 4:18

May the God of hope fill you with all joy and peace, as you trust in Him, so that you may overflow with hope by the power of the Holy Spirit. —Romans 15:13

Did you wake up to another hopeless day today? Maybe the problems seem too big to handle, the money is too sparse to stretch, the children are still out of control, and the court appearance is approaching. Well, against all hope, *hope!*

Abraham could have given up on the promise God spoke to him. He was an old man, his wife was old, and yet God said He had a plan for them. God promised Abraham a son with his 90-year-old wife and said he would be the father of many nations. It was an impossible promise with an unbelievable outcome. Abraham waited, and the years passed. He got older, and Sarah got older, so he tried to make the promise come to pass in his own way. He caused himself more problems because he didn't want to wait for God's timing or believe God could do the impossible.

The book of Romans shows us the real heart of Abraham. Against all hope, when it seemed absolutely impossible, Abraham believed! We cannot let circumstances keep us from believing God has an answer for us and a promise for a better day. Even if today is a tough one, choose to keep hope. God is making a miracle for you—believe that, hope in that, and wait for it to come. Don't become despondent when it doesn't happen fast enough for you. I know it's hard, but it's a choice only you can make. Abraham was richly rewarded because he chose to hope rather than give up. God wants to bless you as well. God's timing is rarely ours, but His timing is always perfect.

~

Hope is what gives us life and a reason to live. When my hope was stripped away, my desire to live went with it. I enjoyed nothing, looked forward to nothing, and cared about nothing. It was a miserable way to exist. When I chose to hope in the faithfulness of Christ to make my life better, even when I couldn't see how God could do it, I was rescued from the pit of the living dead—hopelessness. When we choose hope, we receive life.

Day 19—Choose to plan for your future

Know also that wisdom is like honey for you: If you find it, there is a future hope for you, and your hope will not be cut off. —Proverbs 24:14

If you are wise, your wisdom will reward you; if you are a mocker, you alone will suffer. —Proverbs 9:12

To seek wisdom means we must let go of the foolish things in our lives. Ask yourself today who or what has kept you from fulfilling your dreams, from moving forward with your life, or from making you a better you. It could be you, yourself.

An undisciplined person will float through life each day without planning, studying, or preparing for anything better or new. A wise person will continuously evaluate her goals, strategize to attain them, and then do the work it takes to accomplish them.

If you woke up hating the thought of going to your job today, begin to look for other job opportunities. I know it's not easy to find a new job, it can be intimidating and scary. However, when we seek the wisdom of God, we have His favor when applying. If you stay in your current job, remember to be the best employee possible! A dependable, on-time person with a good-natured attitude is often rewarded with promotions.

What is one personal goal you would like to attain? Think

about it today. Just choose one. Your future can just happen, or you can begin to take control of your life and plan how you'd like your future to look. Take one step today to prepare for tomorrow.

~

One day, my pastor asked me what I enjoyed doing. I had no answer for him. All I knew was housework, childcare, and working at any job that would put food on our table. I had no idea what I personally liked to do anymore. After thinking and praying, I realized I really wanted to go to a Christian college and study the Bible. It seemed odd and frivolous, but, I chose to take one class and discovered how much I loved it. That class was the beginning of a call to become a minister. I didn't start out with that goal, I just took a step toward something I wanted to do. That might be a good place for you to start as well.

Day 20—Choose your friends wisely

One who has unreliable friends soon comes to ruin, but there is a friend who sticks closer than a brother. —Proverbs 18:24

Friends are important to our mental and physical well-being. Do your friends challenge you to become a better person? Are they people you respect? If you are surrounding yourself with friends who feed your anger, laziness, or bad habits, it's time for you to choose new friends.

Letting go of a friend can be a hard thing to do, but today is the day for you to evaluate your friends. Make a list if you must. Write down the pros and cons of your friendships. If there are people who are detrimental to your mental or spiritual growth, those who either encourage or enable your destructive habits, you must let them go. (This may or may not be permanent, but until they no longer influence you, separation is the only solution.)

Figuring out how and where to find new friends can be difficult. School and church groups can be a good place to start if your workplace is not an option. Volunteer, even once a month, somewhere that can give you a new base for friendships.

Your friends will either help you grow toward your goals or keep you from them. Which would you prefer?

Today, evaluate your friends. Tomorrow, begin to make new choices about them.

When I was young, I had a best friend. We were inseparable. When we reached ninth or tenth grade, she began to change. She wanted to date a boy, but her parents didn't want her dating. Soon we were going to a movie or roller rink only to meet up with her boyfriend. I had become entangled in her lies and deceit and finally decided I no longer wanted to be part of her life of deception. I didn't want to be used, and I wanted to regain my self-respect. It was incredibly hard to lose that friendship, but it was one of the wisest choices I've ever made. My friend continued to lie and manipulate and ended up a very unhappy adult with many problems. And I could have been at her side had I not chosen to find new friends and let go of the friend who's life goals and integrity no longer matched mine.

Day 21—Choose to protect your home

Love does not delight in evil but rejoices with the truth. It always protects, always trusts, always hopes, always perseveres.
—1 Corinthians 13:6–7

I hope your home is a safe place for you and for your children today. If, however, you feel threatened, or your children are at risk, today is the day to choose to protect your home.

Your friends and others you have relationships with should be people of integrity, care, and love. If they are explosive in behavior, unable to control their drinking, or are using drugs, your home is not a place of *truth, protection, trust, or hope.*

Friends, family, and the church can help you make wise choices, but only you can uphold your decisions. Your children need you, as the parent, to love them enough to keep them safe and not put them in harm's way. Children living in homes where they are abused or living in fear can become rebellious or angry and often turn to gangs, drugs, or crime as a form of escape.

Protecting your home may involve legal action, a move, or breaking off a relationship you've been hoping would get better. Try to find someone who will stand with you, pray with you, and give you wise counsel through this process. Having God and a trusted friend in your corner can give you strength to do the things you cannot do on your own.

Choose today to protect your home and family from danger.

~

I remember a woman who came to my office for counseling. She wasn't from our church, so I think she felt safe asking us for help. We had several sessions together, and we were making progress in her ability to finally recognize healthy behavior from unhealthy words and actions in her home. One day she said, "I realized yesterday that every time my boyfriend and I get in an argument, I know it will end with him taking out his gun as he threatens to kill himself. This is normal for our home. That's not really normal though, is it?" She wasn't even sure this behavior wasn't normal or unsafe. She hadn't even considered he could turn the gun on her instead of himself. Sometimes we live in a dangerous situation so long we don't even realize how bad it's gotten, or we just don't know how to escape. We, and our children, deserve to live in peace, without threats or fear. This woman chose to ask for help, and a way of escape.

Day 22—Choose to learn something new today

. . . let the wise listen and add to their learning, and let the discerning get guidance. —Proverbs 1:5

It's important to continue your education, learn new job skills, and explore new hobbies. Keeping our minds active and engaged does a number of things for our health and well-being.

It keeps our minds sharp, takes the focus off our problems, improves job and promotion opportunities, allows us to keep in step with our children, and encourages us to stretch our goals.

Guidance comes from someone who has proven herself to be a solid person in the areas you desire to strengthen in your own life. It may be in self-discipline, cooking, parenting techniques, decision-making, budgeting, or study. She may or may not be a family member, but she should be someone who believes in you and has patience and wisdom to teach without lecturing.

Today, write down a topic or hobby you want to explore more deeply and begin to think about potential mentors and areas of growth.

My first goal was to begin a course of study, but I was sure I would absolutely fail the first class I took. Because I had failed at my marriage and had come to believe I was always wrong, my confidence was at rock bottom.

My pastor and his wife were my mentors in this area. They encouraged me, gave me advice about where and how to begin taking the classes I desired, and they were my cheerleaders, always confident I could do it!

I took my first correspondence course and bravely worked through it. My mentors were very close during that first course, but as my confidence gradually increased, I needed their input less and less. I also found that, in the midst of learning new things and expanding my mind, my problems ceased to be all-consuming.

Go after your dream by continuing your studies!

Day 23—Choose to say something nice about someone you don't like

Those who consider themselves religious and yet do not keep a tight rein on their tongues deceive themselves, and their religion is worthless. —James 1:26

But I tell you, love your enemies and pray for those who persecute you, that you may be children of your Father in heaven — Matthew 5:44

As Christians we are supposed to love everyone, but in reality, some people rub us the wrong way and are difficult to be around. There are also those who have hurt us or our children. Do we have to love them, too? According to this scripture, yes, but in a biblical manner. But what does that mean?

God loves everybody, and because God's Spirit now lives in us, we are called to love everyone too, even our enemies. However, God doesn't want you to put yourself in harms way or subject yourself to abuse—that would be foolish. So then, what does "love your enemies" mean in real life? Don't become like your enemy in words or actions, but remain faithful to God's character of Love. Speak kind words, or don't say anything at all. The book of James tells us that only the Holy Spirit can control our tongues, and Matthew tells us not to take on the character of our enemies by acting the way they do.

Your enemy may be a spouse, a family member or a coworker. It doesn't really matter. The extent of their hurt or abuse may run deep, but you cannot dwell on it or surround yourself with people who will perpetuate your anger. This will only cause you to become bitter and mean as well. Change the direction of negative conversations and refuse to jump on the complaint wagon, and your day will become much brighter.

Choosing to be pleasant rather than spiteful will help you maintain joy, bring healing, and restore your peace.

Today, choose to say something nice to, or about, someone you don't like, and see what a difference it makes in *you*.

~

Hurtful words can come from many sources. When I had "Christians" saying hurtful things to me or about me, I had to ignore their presumptions and control my tongue. I didn't defend myself or argue, I just let my attitude and actions define my character. Single moms are often stereotyped in hurtful ways. Let your words, decisions, and life speak louder than words of anger or defense. This goes for the exes in your life as well (in-laws included). Don't think I'm perfect. I used to get mad and say things I'd like to take back. However, as I matured in my faith, I realized praying for my enemies and persecutors took them off my hands and put them in to God's. It was actually calming and brought me even closer to God.

Day 24—Choose to eat healthy

Do not join those who drink too much wine or gorge themselves on meat, for drunkards and gluttons become poor, and drowsiness clothes them in rags. —Proverbs 23:20-21

If asked, "Do you want to be healthy?" wouldn't you answer "Yes"? Did you know your eating and drinking habits strongly affect your attitude and emotions? Too much sugar can cause hyperglycemia, which affects the brain with confusion, depression, personality changes, and impaired reason (it also makes us sluggish and tired and unmotivated!). Lack of fruits and vegetables affects our teeth, gums, and digestive system. Processed and fried foods not only clog arteries, but also affect liver function. I'm not a health food fanatic—these are just known facts about how our body processes the foods we eat.

With all this knowledge, why do we still eat so poorly? Maybe one or more of these reasons has become your excuse:

- It's been a long work day and you didn't plan a meal.

- You think cooking is too much work—fast food is just easier.

- You think it's too expensive to eat healthier.

- You don't know how to cook or purchase the right foods.

- You've lost interest in how you look or feel.

Those are all realities of life, but try replacing those excuses with healthier choices. Think of cooking as a hobby instead of a chore. Cook some meals with your kids—this is a great teaching time and can be so much fun. Find a retired relative, church member, or friend who would love to share their cooking knowledge and skills with you. Visit mayoclinic. com and search for "healthy diet."

Today, make plans for one healthy meal choice, eliminate one regular bad habit food, and choose to begin a healthier eating routine for you and your family. Eating healthy can be a joy!

~

I went through a period of years when I constantly had a break out and my face was red and sore. The doctors just kept saying it was hormonal changes caused by my pregnancies. One day, by chance, I read an article about Candida, and realized I had many of the symptoms. I stopped eating sugar and yeast for three weeks, and for the first time in eight years, my face cleared up and I began to feel better. We don't always realize how much our diet affects so many aspects of our health and emotions. Taking the time to research healthier food choices, without becoming obsessed, will be worth your while.

Day 25—Choose to exercise

Everyone who competes in the games goes into strict training. They do it to get a crown that will not last; but we do it to get a crown that will last forever. —1 Corinthians 9:25

As single parents, our race is not a sprint, but a marathon obstacle course! Our prize is the joy of seeing our children grow into well-adjusted and healthy adults. We need strength and endurance to run this race, moms! That means exercise.

Every year Camp Pendleton Marine Base opens it doors to the community for its Annual Mud Run. This is a difficult course to run because of its many obstacles. It's best to run with a partner who can help you over the walls and up the hills. Runners are exhausted by the time they reach the final mud pit. I once watched this race as a friend of mine competed, and I was amazed as the winner crossed the finish line. It was not a young, buff contender, but an elderly man in his mid-60s who won. This man had obviously chosen a life of disciplined exercise that allowed him to win a race against all odds.

As single parents, we have a hard race to run as well, and sometimes the obstacles seem impossible to hurdle. How do we muster the desire and discipline required when we are exhausted before we begin? How do you tell yourself "No more excuses" when it comes to exercising?

You must first keep your eye on the prize and remember

your goals: a healthy family life, the ability to deal rationally with life's problems, and the ability to run the race of life well. These will give you the drive needed to exercise and be disciplined.

You must also choose an exercise routine that works for you and your family.

Begin with something easy and attainable like a short walk after work or quick stretching routine in the morning. If it's enjoyable, you'll increase your time and routine. You'll lose all interest if you overdo it. Let your kids walk (or bike) with you—push a stroller, talk and bond with them! Be creative and find an exercise routine that works for you.

Today make the choice that you will begin to exercise, look for a practical workout that fits your schedule, and begin doing *something* by the end of this week.

~

I once called my doctor, sure I was dying of something. I had no energy, I was tired all the time, and my mind felt muddled. She said, "I know you're already tired, but you need to walk. It will relieve the stress and actually increase your energy level." As a single mom with five kids, I thought she was crazy. However, I began to take a short walk when I got home from work. Sometimes I would throw food into the oven to bake and then walk. I was shocked at the difference it made.

Day 26—Choose to change a bad habit

Don't become so well-adjusted to your culture that you fit into it without even thinking. Instead, fix your attention on God. You'll be changed from the inside out. Readily recognize what He wants from you, and quickly respond to it. Unlike the culture around you, always dragging you down to its level of immaturity, God brings the best out of you, develops well-formed maturity in you. —Romans 12:2 (The Message)

We all have bad habits. It may be impatience, yelling at your kids, being consistently late, not keeping your home clean and presentable, lazy cooking or eating habits . . . the list can be exhaustive, but it's not unchangeable.

Today pick one bad habit that you really would like to eliminate from your life. With the Lord's help, we can rid ourselves of our bad habits, one by one.

First, if you're angry, make sure unforgiveness is not the cause of your short-tempered responses. Go back to the devotional on forgiveness and give your hurts and anger to God. Let Him be the judge and record keeper. Forgiveness brings amazing peace and eliminates many poor reaction habits.

Second, don't make excuses for your bad habit. None. Begin to look for ways to correct and change it. Give yourself a time-out before responding to a situation if your temper gets the best of you. Pray and seek the Lord, then respond.

Think about what you're teaching your children through your bad habit. Are you teaching that laziness is okay and excusable? Are you teaching them that poor eating habits come from lack of budget when it's really a lack of discipline and planning? Are you teaching that yelling is an appropriate response when things don't go the way you want? Our lives are a living example (don't go down the guilt road now—don't look back, just begin to make changes).

To change a bad habit, there can be no more excuses and no more laziness. It's time to become the adult and raise your children the way they deserve by breaking destructive personal and family habits.

Today is the day to consider one bad habit your want to eliminate. Write it down, bring it the Lord for His help, list practical ways to begin breaking the habit, become accountable to someone who will help and encourage you, and be grateful that God gives you the opportunity to say "the old has gone, the new has come" (2 Corinthians 5:17) in every aspect of your life!

~

My first major bad habit change came when I decided not to argue with my kids about discipline. I would only give them one warning—one! Then I had to follow through with the discipline I had told them to expect. They learned to be responsible for their choices and actions, and I learned that my follow through eliminated the need to scream.

*Day 27—*Choose to say something nice about yourself

May these words of my mouth and this meditation of my heart be pleasing in your sight, LORD, my Rock and my Redeemer. —Psalm 19:14

I praise You because I am fearfully and wonderfully made; Your works are wonderful, I know that full well.—Psalm 139:14

Wow, that should be easy! However, for many single mothers, it is very difficult to find any positive trait in themselves. We recognize our shortcomings, but rarely our gifts or talents. So today you need to find something nice to say about yourself and not utter one self-deprecating word.

If you can read the book *Telling Yourself the Truth* by William Backus and Marie Chapian, it will dramatically change your self-image. This book uses Scripture to describe your beauty and value. Every woman who has been belittled, put down or ridiculed, or believes she's ugly or unlovable should hear these truths. You will begin to see yourself differently when you look through God's eyes and not the eyes of others— or even your own. The characteristics of value, worth, and beauty will also be passed on to your children as they see you become confident in your value.

If you think you have ugly hair, save up enough money to get one really nice professional haircut. If you've been told you are stupid, take a class and prove to yourself that you are not.

Are you gentle, kind, compassionate? Do you work hard, love, and care for the needs of your kids? Are you generous and giving, despite your own needs? As you focus on your strengths, your weaknesses will begin to fade away.

Find something nice to say about yourself today, especially in an area you feel vulnerable. Say it out loud!

~

Oh my, this was a hard one for me. I felt ugly, unlovable, and stupid. How I got there, I don't know, but I believed it to be true. It took a lot of effort for me to find one small thing on which to compliment myself. My character was much easier to compliment than my looks. I still struggle with this, but I learned the power of my words when I began to speak positive things about myself instead of negative. My self-esteem changed dramatically when I began to view myself through God's eyes, and chose pleasing words to describe myself.

Day 28—Choose to take control of your finances

Again, it will be like a man going on a journey, who called his servants and entrusted his property to them. To one he gave five talents of money, to another two talents, and to another one talent, each according to his ability. Then he went on his journey. The man who had received the five talents went at once and put his money to work and gained five more. So also, the one with the two talents gained two more. But the man who had received the one talent went off, dug a hole in the ground and hid his master's money. —Matthew 25:14–18

Whether you have little or much, it's been given to you by God. He has given you money to manage well and wisely. I know that's easier said than done, but the less you have, the more you need to take control of your spending choices.

I would tell you to make a budget spreadsheet listing all of your income and all of your expenses, but you've probably already done that (if not, you should). The problem comes with following through on your budget. Here are just a few basic ideas to get you started on the road to living within your means:

- Buy groceries that will go farther than a frozen meal or snack.

- Use a credit card only if you can pay the balance when the bill comes due.

- Plan ahead for back-to-school purchases. Start on that list at the beginning of the summer so you don't have to purchase everything at once.

- By adding a rent or life insurance policy to your auto insurance policy you may actually reduce your payments (a multi-policy is often cheaper than a single policy).

- If you only use cash, make envelopes for each of your weekly/monthly expenses. For example, make a separate envelope for groceries, utilities, rent, insurance, etc. Do not use this cash for other spontaneous purchases.

- Tithing makes no sense in the natural, but money always seems to stretch farther when you tithe (it's a godly principle).

- Always save something, even just $5–10, from each paycheck.

- Avoid impulse buying, especially when feeling depressed or trapped.

Today, spend wisely and responsibly. Make an appointment with someone who can help you get your bills under control and paid off and help you gain financial freedom.

~

I literally had fifteen cents when my husband left me. I didn't know how I would buy groceries or pay the rent. Thank goodness I had always been good with money—it helped me a lot—but I know what it feels like to have none. I applied for a credit card to establish credit (not to charge things!). One company finally gave me one, and I purchased a small $10 item and paid it off when the bill came. I did this regularly for several months. By the time I was ready to purchase a car, I had established credit and I was given the small loan I needed for my cheap little car. I cooked hot dishes that were cheap, but filling. I wrote out menus and grocery lists that I didn't vary from once I got to the store. With determination, you can get your finances under control and have peace of mind.

Day 29—Choose not to worry

Therefore I tell you, do not worry about your life, what you will eat or drink; or about your body, what you will wear. Is not life more than food, and the body more than clothes? Look at the birds of the air; they do not sow or reap or store away in barns, and yet your heavenly Father feeds them. Are you not much more valuable than they? Can any one of you by worrying add a single hour to your life? —Matthew 6:25–27

So do not fear, for I am with you; do not be dismayed, for I am your God. I will strengthen you and help you; I will uphold you with my righteous right hand. —Isaiah 41:10

When your eyes popped open this morning, did your worrying begin? We all have things to worry about, but worries are multiplied for single mothers. We carry all of the responsibility, make all of the decisions, and feel responsible for everyone and everything. This scripture reminds us that all of our worrying won't change anything. Nothing! But how do we stop?

We stop by believing God is with us and will help us face all our fears. God is in control, not us.

Are your fears and worries real or imagined (possible, but not probable)? Will your worrying bring a solution or resolve to the issue? Constant worry is destructive and divisive. It causes illness in our bodies and can separate us from our children, family, and friends. You must make a choice to trust God instead of worry about everything. Bad things can happen, but if you constantly worry about the improbable possibilities, you will have no peace.

So today, say these words out loud: "God is in control, I am not. I trust God to take care of me, and my children. I choose to let my irrational worry control me no longer. I choose to seek help from someone who can help me with the real problem I'm facing and worried about." Take action to solve the things you can, and give the rest to God. I know it's hard, but choose to trust God today and worry less.

~

I worried about too many things for too many years. I still struggle with worry and have to go back to trusting God and letting go. I had real fears I worried about, but I had many more possible fears I worried about. A friend once asked me, "How many of your fears have ever come to pass?" Umm. . . "Few to none." But how many hours, days, and weeks did I spend worrying about those fears? Too many! I'm far from perfect, but I'm much better at worrying less and trusting God more—letting go of the things that are out of my control and looking for solutions to the things that I can change. Worry is a destructive companion to single mothers, yet we all tend to cuddle up with it.

Day 30—Choose to have a day of rest

. . . But they rested on the Sabbath in obedience to the commandment. —Luke 23:56

There is a reason God said we need to have a day of rest. Our health and well-being are diminished when we push and push and push until we finally collapse. You may be saying, "Who will do the work if I don't? There is no one else, and the work must get done." Maybe everything won't get done, but you can make wise choices about what really needs to be done and what doesn't. Either way, you need a day of rest.

Today may not be your day of rest, but you need to have one scheduled *and kept* this week. Think about what you could do on that day of rest. Take your kids to the park, play a game with them, take a nap, read a book, go for a walk. Do something peaceful and calming.

Organizing your day can relieve a lot of daily stress too. Even if there is a lot on your to-do list, don't push yourself until the wee hours of the morning—you need your sleep! Pushing for perfection and over-extending yourself is how you can begin to lose relationship with your children—you know, those kids you're doing all this work for. You can become so tired and crabby they won't even want to be around you. Lighten up and relax a little each day—it is possible. I had five kids and worked like crazy, so I know it's possible. It's a choice.

Be careful about procrastination as well—it causes frustration for everyone. Peace will follow a steady work pace, but not a frenzied one. There will always be unexpected interruptions and added chores in your day, but keep in mind that very few things are life-threatening. We do have a lot of work that needs to be done, but ruining your health trying to meet unrealistic expectations (that you usually put on yourself) is not the way God desires you to live.

Even if this is not your day of rest, try taking a bubble bath tonight and relax just for you!

Today, work wisely and begin to make plans for your day of rest for this week.

~

When I first had to go back to work, I was frantically trying to keep the same cleaning standards I had as a stay-at-home mom. All I did was work, and I never seemed to rest. I was driving myself, and my family, crazy. Somehow I believed a clean house defined me as a good mom. I finally settled into a place of sanity and told the kids we would keep the kitchen, bathroom, and living area presentable during the week and do a thorough cleaning of everything once a week. I closed the bedroom doors and we all lived happily every after. We can't do it all—we can only do our best while trying to keep a sense of harmony in our homes. Taking a day of rest keeps our life in balance.